SNOW WHITE

A full-length adaptation from

The Brothers Grimm

by

MICKEY COBURN

Copyright Mickey Coburn 1985

Published By

Blue Moon Plays

For That Once-In-A-Lifetime Blue Moon Experience

<u>Snow White</u>, by Mickey Coburn, Copyright © 1985
All rights reserved.

CAUTION: Professionals and amateurs are hereby warned that performance of <u>Snow White</u> is subject to payment of a royalty unless written permission is given waiving such fee. The Play is fully protected under the copyright laws of the United States of America, and of all countries covered by the International Copyright Union (including the Dominion of Canada and the rest of the British Commonwealth), and of all countries covered by the Pan-American Copyright Convention, the Universal Copyright Convention, and the Berne Convention, and of all countries with which the United States has reciprocal copyright relations. All rights, including professional/amateur stage rights, motion picture, recitation, lecturing, public reading, radio broadcasting, television, video or sound recording, all other forms of mechanical or electronic reproduction, such as CD-ROM, CD-I, DVD, information storage and retrieval systems and photocopying, and the rights of translation into foreign languages, are strictly reserved. Particular emphasis is placed upon the matter of readings, permission for which must be secured from the Author in writing. Anyone receiving permission to produce the Play is required to give credit to the Author as sole and exclusive Author of the Play on the title page of all programs distributed in connection with performances of the Play and in all instances in which the title of the Play appears for purposes of advertising, publicizing or otherwise exploiting the Play and/or a production thereof. Author's name must be one-third the size of the title.

ISBN: 978-1-943416-39-4
Published by Blue Moon Plays, LLC
4876-118 Princess Anne Road #208
Virginia Beach, VA 23462-4499
Phone: 757-816-1164
Printed in the USA
Cover: Margaret McSeveney
Editor: Jean Klein

CHANGES TO SCRIPT - Copyright law prevents this script from being copied or altered in any way by any technical or digital means. There may be no changes made to the script including but not limited to casting or dialogue without permission of the publisher and/or playwright.
Video Taping - One video tape may be made for archival purposes only.
Livestreaming - Livestreaming is permissible with an additional fee.

PERFORMANCE/STAGED READING OF SCRIPT

This script is licensed for production by blue moon plays. It may NOT be performed or read aloud in any way (with or without admission fees) in a classroom, around a table, in front of a non-paying audience without a performance fee, which varies.

For any performance, you must apply for and purchase performance rights: in class, in school, for educational purposes, for paying or nonpaying audiences of any size, as a concert reading or a staged reading.

Anyone receiving permission to produce the Play is required to give credit to the Author as sole and exclusive Author of the Play on the title page of all programs distributed in connection with performances of the Play and in all instances in which the title of the Play appears for purposes of advertising, publicizing or otherwise exploiting the Play and/or a production thereof. Author's name must be one-half the size of the title.

All performances and/or readings of this script, whether or not admission fees are required, must apply for and receive a Performance License. There is a flat 100 fee if you wish to live stream performance.

Special Considerations:
Small-group readings around a table or in the classroom:
- If you are planning to use this script FOR CLASSROOM USE, you must purchase scripts for the members of your class or group. These may be purchased as a downloadable PDF (class/group study pack) which may be printed for that class only.
- If you are a small group doing private play readings for YOUR OWN ENTERTAINMENT or for a SMALL SENIOR ACTIVITY GROUP, you must purchase the number or scripts required by the characters: these may be purchased as a multi-copy download which will give you a printable script that you may copy for that reading only.

- Digital versions cannot be added to a free or paid online library or website, in any format, with or without member access, without the publisher's permission.

TO PERFORM THIS PLAY

You must buy sufficient scripts for the cast + 3, apply for performance rights, pay the performance fee, and receive a performance license.

To purchase scripts:

- Purchase sufficient printed hard copies (one for each cast member, plus 3 for the crew) - an automatic 10 percent discount is applied to multiple printed hardcopies at the point of ordering.

or

- Purchase a Multicopy PDF which allows you to print sufficient copies of this script (one for each cast member, plus 3 for the crew). Click Return to Merchant to download your printable PDF. A link to the download will also be emailed to you, along with a link to the application for performance license.

To apply for a Performance License, go to the Product Page of the play and fill out and submit the application form.

To pay the Performance Fee, simply pay the invoice you will be emailed when we receive your application for performance.

Your Performance License for your requested dates will be emailed to you. All scripts and licenses shall be obtained at Blue Moon Plays at www.havescripts.com

If you wish to make changes in the script of any kind, you must receive permission from the publisher or the playwright. Permission is usually granted readily when schools or theaters face casting problems and the changes do not affect the quality or intent of the original.

For information, visit www.havescripts.com;
email info@bluemoonplays.com
or call 757-816-1164

Snow White and the Seven Dwarfs

CAST OF CHARACTERS

Lieber Raimund:	The Woodsman/Prince
Snow White:	The Princess
Walpurga	
Gerhardina Belechech:	The Queen
Eudoxia:	The Mirror
Euphemia	
Hedwig	The Siamese Cat
Flogelind	The Bird
Sussig	The Skunk
Misha	The Lion
Frithmund	The Prince/Huntsman
Petrus	The Henchman
Mandel	The Seven Little Men
Mertel	
Werther	
Wenzel	
Stoffel	
Steffel	
Fritz	
Sprinzchen	The Jolly Hag
Fritzinn	The Silly Hag
Sigismonda	The Ugly Hag

SETTING

ACT I

	Prologue	Somewhere in the Woods
	Scene 1	Walpurga's Chamber
	Scene 2	The Magical Forest
	Scene 3	Walpurga's Chamber
	Scene 4	Somewhere in the Woods
	Scene 5	The Dangerous Woods
	Scene 6	The Circle of Night
	Scene 7	The Glen
		(Walpurga's Dungeon)

ACT II

	Scene 1	Somewhere in the Woods
	Scene 2	The Glen
	Scene 3	The Circle of Night
		Walpurga's Dungeon
	Scene 4	The Glen
	Scene 5	Walpurga's Dungeon
	Scene 6	The Glen
	Scene 7	The Circle of Night
	Scene 8	The Crystal Lake

Snow White and the Seven Dwarfs

ACT I
PROLOGUE

(*Music. Leafy projection on front curtain Spotlight on **Raimund***)

Raimund: I haven't passed through these woods since I was a very little boy. I'm Lieber Raimund. I used to travel here with my father. He thought this forest was enchanted. He told me about Queen Faustina who was always kind to him. You may have heard of her. They say she sat at her window doing her embroidery in its ebony wood frame, watching the falling snow. She pierced her finger, and when she saw how bright and red the little drops of blood looked on the snow, she said, "I wish I had a child wit skin as white as snow, lips as red as blood and hair as black as ebony." Not long after she ha a baby daughter. She named her Shnei Weiss – Snow White. But we never saw Faustina again because when the Princess was born, the good queen died. When the King remarried, he brought his beautiful new Queen to live with Snow White in his castle in Faustina's magical forest, while he rules the land from his city palace. I haven't passed through these woods since I was a little boy. I've been warned that now it's dangerous and terrible. But I promised my father I'd find Snow White. No one's seen the princess since she was very small. She's somewhere in the dark castle where Queen Walpurga Gerhardina Belechech rules.

(He exits as the curtain opens)

ACT I Scene 1

(**Walpurga**'s chamber; a frightful ambiance; **Hedwig, The Cat** sits on an elegant bench or window seat; a fantastic chair or lounge; the gilded mirror. **The Cat** sings softly)

Hedwig: Magic dark and magic deep –

All that's good has gone to sleep –
Shadows cover up the light –
Queen Walpurga rules the night

(Smoke/fog effect; **Walpurga** *enters.)*

Walpurga : It was a beautiful morning. The sun was glistening through the trees – warm, luxurious, incandescent –
Hedwig: Incandescent – incandescent –
Walpurga: Disgusting!! I have changed all that!! (*thunder cracks)* Now it's gloomy - wonderfully gloomy – dingy – dull!!
Hedwig: Gloomy – gloomy –
Walpurga: Just the way I like it. Hedwig!! Bring me my crown!

*(***Hedwig*** continues to hum while fetching crown & bringing it to **Walpurga**)*

Walpurga: *(sprays herself with perfume from large atomizer)* Oh, horrible – horrible – most horrible!! Ten glorious swans arrived on my crystal lake. All white and graceful and silky!!
Hedwig: (returns, sneezing from the perfume) Grace – grace – ach – ach – choo!
Walpurga: Disgusting!! I have changed all that!! *(thunder cracks)* Now they are ten ugly ducklings – homely, plain, gawky –
Hedwig: (*composed*) Homely – homely –
Walpurga: (*takes the crown and puts it on*) Nothing and nobody will be more beautiful than I!! Nobody!! Eudoxia! Euphemia! Come here!!
Hedwig: Come here – come here –

(The **Mirror**, still until now, comes to her)

Walpurga: Hurry up – hurry up – Hold still. *(fixes crown)* There. Amazing – Splendid – Magnificent!!
Hedwig: Magnificent – magnificent –
Walpurga: Looking glass upon the wall Who's the fairest of us all?
Mirror: Queen of darkness, queen of night –
 Queen who fills the world with fright –
 Enchantress powerful withal—
 You are fairest of us all.

Walpurga: (*laughing wickedly*) True! True! You always speak the truth! You may withdraw. Come, my lovely Hedwig, you'll catch ducklings for your breakfast.
Hedwig: Lovely...lovely...
Mirror: Most powerful of queenlihood
   Two strangers roam within your wood.
Walpurga: (*spinning around and sending Hedwig flying*) Two what? Roam where?
Hedwig: What? What??
Mirror: Most powerful of queenlihood Two strangers….
Walpurga: I heard you the first time!! No one dares to enter my forest – you must be mistaken.
Mirror: We speak the truth so be convinced – One's a huntsman, one a prince.
Walpurga: Who are they? Speak! Speak!
Hedwig: Speak! Speak!
Mirror: One – a huntsman – lost his way
   Because you stole the light of day.
Walpurga: And the other?? Speak!
Hedwig: Speak! Speak!
Walpurga: (*to **Hedwig***) Shut up!
Hedwig: Shut up! ...whoops!

(***Walpurga** lifts her hand ominously; **Hedwig** creeps away cowering*)

Walpurga And the other?
Mirror: The other – strong and wise and bright
   Is looking for the child – Snow White.
Walpurga: Huntsman? Prince? Looking for Snow White! We must stop this immediately!!
Hedwig: (*softly; tentatively*) Immediately….immediate….
Walpurga: (*shouting*) Petrus!! Petrus come here at once. Petrus!! That knave is never here when I want him. (*she gestures – a puff of smoke*) Petrus!

(***Petrus** enters, disoriented; then cow-towing to **Walpurga***)

Petrus: What? What happened? Oh – your majesty – your magnificence – your regalness – your –

Walpurga: Enough!! Where were you when I called? Never mind!
Hedwig: (*confidence returning*) Never mind! Never mind –
Walpurga: There are two strangers in my forest. How could you let this happen?
Petrus: But I....
Walpurga: Never mind! If it weren't for my magic mirror I would have no help at all!
Petrus: But your majesty, I –
Walpurga: Never mind! Go find this intruder who looks for Princess Snow White. Lead him astray. Lose him. Get rid of him!
Petrus: Yes, your majesty –
Walpurga: I will conjure a lion to hunt the huntsman – (**Petrus** *remains*) Well? Are you going?
Petrus: How will I recognize him, your majesty? What does he look like?
Walpurga: He looks like a prince. Surely you can recognize a prince! Dumbkopf! Go!! (**Petrus** *exits*) Come Hedwig. We have work to do –
(***Walpurga** exits followed by **Hedwig***)

Mirror: (*singing*) Magic deep and magic dark
 Strangers roam Walpurga's park
 A lion soon will be at bay –

ACT I Scene 2

(*The Magical Forest.* ***Flogelind** and **Sussig** run in and out followed by **Snow White**. **Snow White**'s dance. At the end of the dance, **Flogelind** re-enters.*)
Flogelind: Princess – princess – a stranger's coming!! A stranger! Quickly – let's hide – he may be a huntsman.
Sussig: Don't worry – I'll protect you – I'll knock him down – I'll beat him up – I'll toss him out –
Flogelind: He's coming – here he comes –
Sussig: Yikes!! (*runs off*)

(***Flogelind** takes **Snow White** off. **Frithmund** enters*)

Frithmund: At last! Daylight! It's dark everywhere in these wood – except here. This is the strangest forest. I hear birds, but I never

see them. I see little animals, but when I come near them they disappear. A moment ago, I thought I heard music. *(calling off)* Hello! Hello!
Flogelind: *(off)* Hello!
Frithmund: Hello!
Flogelind: Hello!
Frithmund: Who are you?
Flogelind: Who are you?
Frithmund: I wonder if it's an echo. (calling) I can't see you!
Flogelind: I'm hiding! (giggles off)
Frithmund: Come out here! Please? (silence) Hello!!

(**Petrus** enters from behind him)

Petrus Hello.
Frithmund Hello?
Petrus: Hello.
Frithmund: (turning around) Oh, there you are –
Petrus ; What? Who?
Frithmund ; Why were you hiding?
Petrus: Who? What?
Frithmund: (looking off) This is very peculiar. *(giggles off stage)*
Petrus: Have you seen a lion?
Frithmund: A lion? No – thank goodness. Wait – there're no lions in this part of the world.
Petrus: *(aside)* Then he must be the Prince. The lion is hunting the huntsman. Your highness –
Frithmund: Excuse me?
Petrus: I'm Petrus – from the court of Queen Walpurga. I'm to lead y u out of the forest.
Frithmund: I'm Frithmund.
Petrus: At your service.

(They click heels and bow to each other knocking heads together; giggles off stage)

Frithmund: How did you know I was here?
Petrus: What? Who?
Frithmund: Me.
Petrus: Who?

Frithmund: Who? Oh, Frithmund – at your service.

(They click heels again and bow to each other knocking heads together; giggles off stage)

Petrus: Oh – uh – you called?
Frithmund: Who?
Petrus: You.
Frithmund: Oh. This is very confusing.
Petrus: Come –we'll go this way –
Frithmund: But I heard a voice this way –
Petrus: It must have been an echo. Shall we go –
Frithmund: Thank you.

(They are about to bow to each other but stop in time)

Frithmund: *(as they exit)* These are very strange woods. I hear birds but I never see them…. (etc.)

*(**Flogelind** & **Sussig** enter as they exit)*

Sussig: They've gone – it's safe now. (**Snow White** enters)
Snow White: What do you suppose that was all about? Petrus must be up to something.
Flogelind: Queen Walpurga must be up to something. Petrus isn't bright enough to think up anything by himself.
Snow White: Do you think that young man is really a prince?
Sussig: Petrus said so.
Snow White: He didn't look like a prince.
Sussig: Why not? What does a prince look like?
Snow White: I don't know. A little taller? A little more – princely.
Sussig: Probably they come in all different shapes and sizes. (acting out the types) Little fat princes with kingdoms filled with bakeries –
Flogelind: *(laughing)* Tall, skinny princes with wrinkled knees – (imitating one)
Sussig: Big, tough princes who look like wrestlers –
Flogelind: Delicate, graceful princes *(ballets across the stage)*
Snow White: Tall, handsome princes with nice smiles and palaces far away from here –

Flogelind: We'll never know for sure. The Queen won't let anyone travel through this forest.
Sussig: Or visit the castle.
Snow White: That one got into the forest – perhaps another will.
Flogelind: On a white horse –
Sussig: To carry you away –
Flogelind/Sussig: And you'll live happily ever after!
Snow White: You're making fun of me.
Sussig: No, Snow White, we don't mean to….
Flogelind: But with what can we fight Walpurga's power? Dreams?
Sussig: Wishes?
Flogelind: Hopes?
Snow White: But without dreams, wishes, hopes, we'd have nothing at all. Oh, Sussig – Flogelind –

*(Unseen, **Raimund** enters)*

Snow White: Imagine – a great ball filled with sunlight – 100 musicians – beautiful, happy people – laughing, dancing. I come in – as I walk down the golden stairway everyone stops; it's very quiet. The prince meets me at the bottom of the stairs. He takes my hand – the music plays – we dance –

*(She dances with her eyes closed; as she passes **Raimund**, he steps in and dances with her)*

Flogelind/Sussig: *(surprised and frightened)* OHHHHHHH!

*(**Snow White** suddenly stops dancing and breaks away)*

Snow White: Ohhhh!
Raimund: Your highness – Forgive me – I didn't mean to frighten you—
Snow White: *(overlapping)* I was just dreaming and suddenly –
Raimund: It was such a charming dream – I didn't mean to – I'm sorry –
Snow White: *(overlapping)* You startled me. I thought you were –
Raimund: *(overlapping)* I'm truly sorry –
Snow White: ---part of the dream.

(They look at each other)

Snow White: Who are you?
Raimund: Lieber Raimund. *(he bows)*
Snow White: Are you – a prince?
Flogelind: He's a huntsman –
Sussig: A woodsman –
Flogelind: You can tell by his clothes –
Sussig: His boots –
Flogelind: Snow White – we'd better go now –
Raimund: Snow White. I wouldn't harm you. *(to the creatures)* Any of you.
Snow White: It's all right, Flogelind.
Sussig: Your highness –
Snow White: Sussig – it's all right. These are my friends. We're not used to strangers.
Raimund: This is a magical forest, isn't it? It's very lovely.
Snow White: Here – in this clearing Deeper in the forest it's dark and dangerous. We never go there. You mustn't go there. You should leave which ever way you came.
Raimund: I'm not afraid.
Sussig: If the Queen finds out you're here – she has terrible powers.
Flogelind: She'll kill you.
Sussig: Or imprison you.
Flogelind: Or lock you in the circle of night.
Sussig: No one ever leaves her forest.
Snow White: You must go before she discovers you.
Raimund: Will you come with me?
Snow White: I? But I…….

*(The **Lion** creeps in quietly behind **Raimund**)*

Sussig: *(seeing the lion)* Ah – ha --- ah---- ha---ah—ha----
Flogelind: *(seeing lion)* Whatza—whatza—whatza—whatza—
Flogelind/Sussig: Iba—iba-iba-iba----look out!!!!!

*(**Raimund** turns & sees the **Lion**. He reaches slowly for his knife)*

Snow White: *(It doesn't occur to her to be frightened; she approaches the lion)* Oh, what a lovely kitty –where ever did you come from?

*(**Lion** growls; FULGELIND & **Sussig** jump back cowering)*

Snow White: *(petting him)* What's that awful noise? We're not going to hurt you. Now – (she tickles him under the chin)

(**Lion** *tries to growl but it turns into a purr*)

Snow White: There! *(laughing)* You're just an old pussy cat. Now what's your name? *(**Lion** purrs)*
Snow White: Come on – tell me your name – Are you shy? Poor baby. Look – I'm Snow White, and that's Flogelind and Sussig. Ths gentleman is Lieber Raimund. Now, who are you?
Misha: *(bashfully)* Misha.
Snow White: Misha! What a nice name. Where ever did you come from, Misha?
Misha: Queen Walpurga –
Snow White: Oh, a magical lion.
Misha: I'm supposed to….
Flogelind: Kill us all!!
Misha: Hunt the huntsman.
Raimund: Amazing!
Snow White: Misha, you wouldn't do a nasty thing like that – such a sweet kitty. *(She hugs him; he purrs)*
Raimund: Truly amazing. He doesn't frighten you at all.
Snow White: *(standing up; **Misha** rubs against her)* Animals never frighten me. They don't hurt anyone except to protect themselves. People – people frighten me more.

(Thunder cracks)

Snow White: We must go now. Leave the forest – if you can. Queen Walpurga knows you're here. You're in danger.
Raimund: Come with me.

(Thunder cracks)

Snow White: We must go now –
Raimund: I'll wait for you, Snow White. I won't leave without you.
Snow White: *(all overlapping)* Go!
Flogelind: Hurry – save yourself –
Sussig: Go!

Misha: Hurry!
Raimund: I'll wait for you – Snow White. (*They've gone; to himself*) I won't leave without you.

ACT I Scene 3

(***Walpurga**'s chamber;* **Walpurga** *sweeps in with* **Hedwig**; *both in a gay mood*)

Walpurga: Didn't we conjure a beautiful lion, Hedwig? What an enormous growl!
Hedwig: *(imitating lion)* Grrrrr----
Walpurga: More fierce – more fierce –
Hedwig: *(trying harder)* Grrrrrrr----
Walpurga: Louder – meaner – grrrrr---

(**Hedwig** *continues to try overlapping with queen*)

Walpurga: *(clapping her hands)* Yes – that's it! *(petting* **Hedwig***)* A wonderful imitation! *(fetching a huge powder puff)* By now that huntsman has been disposed of and Petrus and the so-called prince are wondering aimlessly through the forest. We've done a fine day's work. Eudoxia! Euphemia! Come here!
Hedwig: Grrrrrr –
Walpurga: Enough of that, Hedwig. Behave yourself. *(She powders her face in the mirror)* There – that's much better –
Hedwig: Grrrrr---
Walpurga: If you don't stop that, I will turn you into a mushroom and fry you in an omelet.
Hedwig: Meow.

Walpurga: *(turning back to her mirror)* Looking glass upon the wall Who's the fairest of us all?
Mirror: Queen of darkness, queen of night
 Queen who fills the world with fright –
 Queen you are of beauty rare –
 But Snow White is above all fair!
Walpurga: *(softly, rage is building)* What did you say?
Mirror: Queen of darkness, queen of night.....
Walpurga: *(overlapping)* No! the last part of it –

Mirror: Queen you re of beauty ra---
Walpurga: (*losing it*) The very last!!!
Mirror: Snow White is above all fair.
Walpurga: (*screams – thunder claps*) Aaaagh!!! How dare you! Snow White is a child!! A puny little girl – Aaaagh!!
Hedwig: She's easily disposed of, your majesty. She may be fair, but she's not powerful – magical –
Walpurga: Above all fair!!!! (*she's having a tantrum*)
Hedwig: (*singing*) The Queen would be most fair instead If Snow White suddenly were dead.
Walpurga: (*interested*) How would I explain it to the King?
Hedwig: Oh, King, our Snow White – young and good – Had an accident in the wood-
Walpurga: Yes – yes! Eudoxia – Euphemia – what has become of the huntsman and the lion?
Mirror: The lion now is Snow White's pet. Huntsman with sorrow is beset.
Walpurga: Disgusting! Where is the fair – the most fair – Snow White?
Mirror: Snow White in her chamber plays With song and dance she fills her days.
Walpurga: How sweet! An end to this – HUNTSMAN!!!

(*Smoke effect. **Raimund** appears. He doesn't know how he got there. Disoriented; confused.*)

Raimund: What? How did I get here? What happened? What's going on?
Hedwig: (*overlapping*) You'd better bow – you'd better bow –
Walpurga: Huntsman!

Raimund: The Queen! (*bowing*) Your majesty. You are most powerful.
Walpurga: And therefore you will obey me! You wish to leave my forest. You will take Snow White into the woods. And when you return – you will bring me her heart.
Raimund: (*appalled*) Your majesty?!
Walpurga: Her heart – huntsman! Or I will lock you in the Circle of Night on the dark side of my magic mirror where only a river of tears can save you.
Hedwig: The circle of night – the circle of night --!

Raimund: But your majesty –
Walpurga: Go. Hedwig will lead you to the "most fair" Snow White. I will await your return. *(She exits)*
Raimund: *(calling after her)* Your majesty – I don't understand – please –
Hedwig: Follow me – follow me – follow me—
Mirror: Queen of darkness, queen of night
Queen who fills the world with right
Happiness and joy's forbade
Queen Walpurga's truly mad!!

*(Curtain closes as **Petrus** & **Frithmund** enter in-1; leafy projection appears on front curtain)*

ACT I Scene 4

*(**Petrus** walks in front; **Frithmund** follows)*

Petrus: *(stops short; **Frithmund** bumps into him)* What was that?
Frithmund: *(nervously)* What? What?
Petrus: I heard footsteps.
Frithmund: I don't hear anything – *(they listen; they walk)*
Petrus: *(stopping short again; **Frithmund** bumps into him again)* Did you hear that?
Frithmund: What? What??

*(**Petrus** takes 3 steps forward; **Frithmund** takes 3 steps forward. they listen. repeat)*

Petrus: Someone's following us.
Frithmund: *(frightened)* You said you'd lead me out of the forest. We've been walking all day. I think we're going in circles –
Petrus: Someone's following us – we'd better hurry –
Frithmund: Petrus – do you know the way out of this forest?
Petrus: Well, of course – I – it's – over there – and through the – and around the other –
Frithmund: Petrus!
Petrus: No.
Frithmund: No what?
Petrus: No. I don't know the way out of the forest. We're lost.

Frithmund: We're lost?
Petrus: We're lost.
Frithmund We're lost.
Petrus: It all looks the same. I don't recognize anything. Besides I have no sense of direction.
Frithmund: *(pushing **Petrus** behind him)* I'll get us out of here. Come on –

*(They walk; **Frithmund** is in front this time; they stop; bump)*

Frithmund: *(listening)* Did you hear that?
Petrus: What? What??
Frithmund: Someone's following us!

(Repeat three steps bit twice)

Frithmund: Yikes! We'd better hurry – this way!!

(They exit as the curtain opens)

ACT I Scene 5

*(The Dangerous Woods. Dimly lit. **Snow White**, **Raimund** discovered)*

Raimund: That's what Queen Walpurga told me to do. Unbelievable as it is.
Snow White: I don't understand. I haven't done anything. Why does she want me to die?
Raimund: She's mad, Snow White. We have to escape.
Snow White: I know she's capable of terrible things. But there's no reason for her to want me dead. I f only could get word to my father.
Raimund: There isn't time for that now. We must escape.
Snow White: We'll have no chance to escape if we're together. If you don't return, she'll kill us both.
Raimund: I have a plan. I'll return. I'll find a dead animal in the woods and bring her its heart. Is there somewhere you can hide in the meantime?
Snow White: I'll try to get to the other side of the forest, out of Walpurga's reach.

Raimund: But it's too dangerous –

Snow White: The animals are my friends. They'll help me.

Raimund: Then go quickly. When Walpurga thinks you're dead, we'll both be safe. I'll follow you as soon as I can.

Snow White: We left so suddenly – Flogelind, Sussig and Misha don't kow what's happened. I'd feel safer if they were with me.

Raimund: I'll tell them and send them to you. Are you sure you'll be all right?

Snow White: We have no other choice, Raimund. We'd better go now.

Raimund: I'll follow you as soon as I can.

Snow White: Good-bye, Raimund.

Raimund: Snow White –

Snow White: Yes?

Raimund: Be careful….

*(He exits **Snow White** begins to run; the SCARY WOODS appear; cruel laughter is heard; mist rises; strange objects fly out at her; **Snow White**, in a dance-like scene, struggles to escape and finally collapses.)*

Snow White: …Raimund! Raimund!! Help me!!

BLACK OUT

ACT I Scene 6

*(The CIRCLE OF NIGHT; **Raimund** appears in darkness in a whirlpool spotlight. As he speaks the moon appears with eyes peering at him)*

Raimund: This is the Circle of Night on the dark side of the magic mirror. I'm locked in and now I'll never find Snow White. I fooled Queen Walpurga with the dead animal's heart. But I couldn't fool the mirror. Walpurga believes Snow White will die in the dangerous forest. And I can't save her. I'll travel in darkness forever unless I find the river of tears, whatever that might be. Somehow – I must escape – somehow – I must find Snow White again.

(Spot goes out. The eyes in the moon remain and then fade.)

ACT I Scene 7

Snow White: *(waking up and looking around)* I'm still alive. I thought I'd never make it through the night. The sun's shining – I don't know how I got to this lovely place. *(she stands up)* All the scary creatures are gone. Oh, the sun's so warm. What a sweet little house. Who could live in it? *(She knocks on the door; there's no answer; she knocks again)* Hello? Hello?? Is anyone there? *(knocks again; tries the door it opens; she goes in)* What a dear place this is. Everything's so tiny – a family of children must live here. It feels so cozy and safe. I wonder if they'd let me stay awhile. This must be outside of Walpurga's forest – nothing like this could exist in the Queen's woods. Oh, I wish Flogelind and Sussig were here. And Misha. And Raimund. What if whoever lives here isn't friendly? What if ... maybe I'd better...

*(She starts to leave; we hear the musical shoes – wooden shoes -- of the seven little men; **Snow White** retreats into the house)*

Snow White: There's no place to hide – what should I – I know – I'll make myself useful. What can I – oh –

(She grabs a broom & starts to sweep; then she polishes the floor with a rag. The 7 little men appear in a choreographed parade. The first is the leader; the seventh, taller than the rest, attempts continually to cover up the fact that he's taller. They have long white beards & all wear pointed hats or hoods and wooden shoes & carry burlap bags filled with something. They chant to the rhythm of their shoes.)

Together: We're the 7 brothers Hoffenstein,
　　　　　We work together in our mine.
　　　　　No one shirks and no one quits

(one at a time)
>Mandel, Mertel, Werther, Wenzel,
>Stoffel, Steffel and Fritz!
>All for one and one for all,
>Against a world that's much too tall;
>We use our brains, we use our wits,

(one at a time)
>Mandel, Mertel, Werther, Wenzel,
>Stoffel, Steffel and Fritz!

>Together through the thick and thin,
>The best of friends, the best of kin,
>A brotherhood of opposites –

(one at a time)
>Mandel, Mertel, Werther, Wenzel,
>Stoffel, Steffel and Fritz!

*(**Mandel** opens the door & goes inside; the others are behind him. He sees **Snow White** & comes out again, forcing the others back.)*

Mandel: We seem to have company.
Others: *(echoing him)* Company? Company?? (etc.)
Mandel: Probably a thief -- or a murderer –
Others: *(hub-bub of alarm)* What ? No! oh --- *(etc.)*
Mertel: (looking into the house) It looks like a girl –
Others: A girl? A what? A who? *(etc.)*

Mertel: *(looking again)* She seems pleasant enough. *(The others crowd to the door to peer in)*
Wenzel: Can she cook?
Werther: Is she somebody or just a peasant girl?
Stoffel: She may have lost her way.
Steffel; She's gonna make more work for us.
Fritz: She's – she's – she's awful pretty.
Others: Pretty?????
Mandel: Let me see –
Mertel: You're right –
Wenzel: Too skinny –
Werther: Her dress is plain.

Stoffel: She looks nice. *(etc. adlibs)*
Stoffel: One of us should go in and find out who she is.
Fritz: *(quickly)* I will!

(They all leer at him; he backs off)

Fritz: *(shrugging)* I would.
Wenzel: I wish she'd come after dinner; there won't be enough for 8.
Mertel: Perhaps she's very nice.
Mandel: Probably she isn't. I'll go in. Unless someone else wants to. *(No response)* That's what I thought. *(He starts to the door; then turns)* Did you say something??

(They all shake their heads. He turns back to the door, then turns back again)

Mandel: We could go back to work for awhile.
Mertel: Perhaps she'll leave in the meantime –
Wenzel: And miss dinner?
Steffel: Work? Again? Ohhhhh –
Werther: And let her muck around our house?
Fritz: She's awful pretty.

(They leer. He backs off.)

Stoffel: Why don't we all go in together. There's safety in numbers.
Others: Good idea
    Fine
    All right – *(etc. adlibs)*

(They line up to go in; each one tries not be first; finally, they are in their usual order.)

Mandel: *(taking a deep breath)* Here we go!!

*(He opens the door; **Snow White** retreats to the other side of the room. They each step out of their shoes as they step into the house. As **Mandel** steps in, he slides on the polished floor; The others follow into a huge 'pig-pile' with appropriate cries of alarm.)*

Snow White: *(rushing to help them up)* Oh dear, I'm so sorry. I polished the floor – I was only trying to help. Are you hurt? *(They scramble to their feet as she tries to help them up)* Here – let me help – you – *(Once on their feet, they stare at her; only **Fritz** smiles; she smiles back; he crunches down to be shorter)* I'm really sorry – I hope no one's hurt. I guess I'd better go now – good day gentlemen.

(She curtsies & hurries outside. They look at each other & then hurry after her, stepping into their shoes outside.)

Stoffel: Wait – Miss – please don't go –
Mertel: We're not hurt – it's all right –
Steffel: At least we don't have to clean the floor –
Wenzel: Can you cook?
Mandel: We might have broken our necks *(They glare at him.)* – but we didn't.
Werther: We're not being very hospitable. But we don't know who you are –
Mandel: Or why you've been slicking up our floors – *(They wait, staring at her.)*
Stoffel: Miss?
Snow White: I'm Snow White.
Werther: The Princess?

*(A hub-bub of reactions; they take off their hats & bow; **Werther** pulls **Fritz**'s hat off & hands it to him; **Fritz** bows; two of his brothers pull him down to their size)*

Snow White: Oh, please, you needn't do that, you see – how can I say this. It sounds so improbable. Someone is trying to kill me. So I ran away. And I found your house, and I wanted to help so you'd let me stay for awhile.
Mertel: You came through the forest alone?
Steffel: It's very dangerous.
Stoffel: You must be very brave –
Wenzel: Or very lucky.
Werther: Who'd want to hurt you, your highness?
Mandel: There's only one person as wicked as that –
Together: Queen Walpurga Gerhardia Belechech – *(They all cough*

trying to say the last name)
Snow White: *(laughing)* How funny you make her name sound!
Wenzel: But she isn't funny. She's terrible – her woods are just beyond those trees. We never dare to cross into them.
Steffel: We'd be in her power. Her evil power.
Mandel: Won't she follow you here?
Stoffel: The Princess is out of Walpurga's woods and out of Walpurga's reach. *(to **Snow White**)* You're safe now.
Snow White: I have some friends who'll be joining me – then we'll travel on together and get word to my father in the city.
Fritz: May she stay with us until her friends come?

(They look at him; then at each other; they huddle, whispering; then separate)

Mandel: It would probably be all right for you to stay – for awhile.
Snow White: *(delighted)* Oh, thank you sir, and you and you and – I don't know your names –
Together: We're the seven brothers Hoffenstein
We work together in our mine
No one shirks and no one quits –
(One at a time)
Mandel, Mertel, Werther, Wenzel
Stoffel, Steffel and Fritz!
Snow White: *(laughing;curtsies)* I'm very pleased to meet you –
Mandel – Mertel – Wer –
Werther: Werther.
Snow White: Werther – Wenzel –
Stoffel: Stoffel.
Steffel: Steffel.
Snow White: Fritz
Together: And Fritz!!

(Two brothers pull him down to their size.)

Snow White What kind of mine do you have?
Mertel: Well, we're digging for coal to sell to the nearby villages –
Mandel: But we don't find any coal –
Steffel: *(tiredly)* We dig and dig and dig –
Wenzel: All we find are big pieces of glass –

Stoffel: Really useless objects.
Snow White: Glass? In a mine?
Mandel: Never any coal. Probably isn't any coal.
Mertel: Perhaps there is – under the glass – so we haul it home and bury it behind the house –
Werther: To dispose of it, you know.
Steffel: We dig and dig and dig –
Fritz: It's very pretty. *(They leer at him)*
Snow White: Is it Fritz? May I see it?

*(**Fritz** opens his bag & pulls out a large sparkling object)*

Fritz: *(handing it to **Snow White**)* Isn't it wonderful?
Snow White: Oh, my yes. It's very wonderful. But it isn't glass.
Together: It isn't glass?
    What is it then?
    What do you mean"
    What could it be?
    It must be glass.
    What did she say?
    What's that?
Snow White: This is a diamond. You must own a diamond mine.

(Improvised exclamations; they go to their bags & look in.)

Mandel: *(bringing her another gem)* Wait – look at another piece. Are you certain?
Snow White: As certain as I can be. Glass doesn't come from a mine. This is harder than crystal. Look – *(She bends down and cuts one stone with the other)* See? One stone cuts into the other. Only diamonds are that strong. You're very wealthy men.
Fritz: *(cheering)* Yay!!!! *(They leer at him; huddle quickly; separate)*
Together: *(cheering)* Yay!!!
Mertel: We can travel the world –
Werther: Buy all kinds of wonderful things –
Wenzel: Eat all kinds of wonderful food –
Steffel: Never have to work again –
Stoffel: Read all the great books –
Mandel: Probably – if they're really diamonds – *(they leer at him)* We could bring Princess Snow White to her father.

Fritz: A celebration!! Let's have a party!!

*(All cheer; lead **Snow White** into the house – stepping out of their shoes – they slide again into a pig pile; they laugh; lights dim. The Queen's evil laughter is heard above theirs; lights on Queen in her dungeon with the **Mirror** & her caldron & **Hedwig**)*

Walpurga: *(laughing)* The huntsman is locked in the Circle of Night; Petrus and that silly prince are lost in the forest; and Snow White is dead somewhere in the darkest woods. And now – Looking glass upon the wall Who's the fairest of us all?
Mirror: Queen of magic beauty rare
  To who no one can compare
  Except for Snow White in the glen
  With the seven little men –
  Snow White is above all fair.
Walpurga: Snow White? Alive? Escaped the huntsman – Escaped the woods? An end to this! Fair – Fair Shnei Veis. I will take care of you myself. You think you have escaped my power. I will bring my power to you!!

*(She laughs; **Hedwig** meows; **Snow White** & the seven little men dance in the little house; a spot on the Queen; a spot on the Celebration.)*

CURTAIN END ACT I

ACT II Scene 1

*(Somewhere in the woods; in-one; leafy projection on front curtain. Enter **Petrus** & **Frithmund** disheveled)*

Petrus: We've been walking for days, Frithmund. I can't go any further without food.
Frithmund: It can't be much further. If we walk straight in any one direction, we have to arrive somewhere.
Petrus: Right.
Frithmund: No, left. We came from the right – if we walk left we'll be walking straight.
Petrus: Right!
Frithmund: No – left, left! Left is straight. Right?
Petrus: If you say so.
Frithmund: I say so. Now, let's go.
Petrus: *(starting behind him)* Right!
Frithmund: *(turns – frustrated)* Now listen, Petrus, you got us lost in the first place. We've been wandering around for days. If we don't eat something we'll die. If something eats us, we'll die If we don't get some rest, we'll die.
Petrus: What's left?
Frithmund: *(pointing off)* That's left and that's the way we're going so we can get out of this horrible forest.
Petrus: Right!
Frithmund: *(seething)* Petrus! If you don't stop saying that ---
Petrus: Just a minute. Don't get upset. We came from the right. Right?
Frithmund: Right.
Petrus: And we're walking that way – to the left – right?
Frithmund: Right.
Petrus: If we walk straight in any one direction, we have to arrive somewhere – right?
Frithmund: Right.
Petrus: And the left is the direction that's left. Right?
Frithmund: Right.
Petrus: So let's go. I don't understand what you're fussing about.
Frithmund: I'm not fussing. I'm – oh, never mind. Come on –
Petrus: Right!!

Frithmund: (chasing him off) What did I tell you? We're going to the left – if we walk straight in any one direction, we have to arrive somewhere ----

(Curtain opens as they exit)

ACT II Scene 2

*(Curtain opens on the glen; **Snow White** is in the house giving a cloth satchel to **Stoffel**; **Fritz** stands nearby; the others are outside getting ready for work – putting on shoes, getting burlap bags ready , etc.)*

Snow White: I packed some extra cakes for Wenzel so he won't be hungry today.
Stoffel: Thank you, Princess. He'll appreciate it.
Mandel: *(near open door)* Wenzel will probably be hungry anyway. He's always hungry.
Mertel: Let's go. The sooner we get our work done, the sooner we'll be home.
Werther: The more work we do, the richer we'll be.
Steffel: Aren't we rich enough? I thought we wouldn't have to work anymore.
Wenzel: May I carry the lunch?
Mandel: If you carry the lunch, it will become breakfast. Stoffel has it.

*(**Stoffel**, **Fritz** & **Snow White** come out of the house.)*

Fritz: I think I should stay here and protect Snow White.
Steffel: If anyone should stay, it's me. I'll protect Snow White.
Werther: You just want to get out of working.
Steffel: That isn't so –
Snow White; Please. I'll be perfectly safe here. No one has to stay with me.
Mertel: What will you do all day?
Mandel: Don't polish the floors –

Snow White: *(laughing)* I promise. I'll never polish a floor again. If you like, I'll bake something.
Wenzel: What?? What??

Stoffel: It'll be a surprise. Come on.
Mandel: Let's go now. *(they line up)* Stay in the house. Don't talk to strangers.

*(They march off singing their song; **Fritz** looking over his shoulder at **Snow White**)*

Snow White: *(waving them off)* Goodbye!

*(**Snow White** goes into the house; finds a bowl & wooden spoon & looks about for things she needs for baking. **Sprinzchen** – the jolly hag – appears, humming a tune)*

Sprinzchen: *(calling as she walks)* Pretties to sell! Pretties to sell! Pretties, pretties, pretties to sell! Yoo hoo – is anyone home? *(She knocks on the door. **Snow White** tentatively opens the top of the door)* Good morning my dear! I have such pretty things for such a pretty girl.
Snow White: Oh, I'm sorry, but I can't talk to strangers.
Sprinzchen: Of course not. You should never talk to strangers. I'm Sprinzchen—from the village. There – now I'm not a stranger. May I come in? I have such dainties to show you.
Snow White: Well, you see, it's not my house.
Sprinzchen: Of course, I understand. It's such a delicious morning, won't you come outside for a moment? Really beauteous things to show you . Such a pretty girl.
Snow White: I guess it couldn't hurt just to look – for a moment. *(she comes out of the house)*
Sprinzchen: *(looking in her basket)* Let me see what Sprinzchen has for you – especially for you. Ahhh – Here it is – for your beautiful, ebony hair. *(she holds up a jeweled comb)*
Snow White: Oh, what a handsome comb. I'd love to buy it, but I have no money to pay with.
Sprinzchen: Oh, that's all right. I know the seven little men very well. You can pay for it another time. I'd really like you to have it, since you love it so well. Here, may I put it in your hair?
Snow White: Oh, yes – please.
Sprinzchen: There – how perfect that is. *(**Sprinzchen** puts the comb in **Snow White's** hair; **Snow White** screams & falls down)* Now, oh, fairest of them all, that is the end of you. *(exits singing & humming)*

*(**Flogelind**, SUSIG & **Misha** are heard off)*

Flogelind: Look – I see a clearing ahead.
Sussig: Oh, thank goodness – thank goodness.
Misha: Even the trees are mean in this forest.

(They enter – bounding in, out of breath)

Flogelind: There – we made it.
Sussig: Finally.
Misha: But we didn't find Snow White on the way. Do you think she's lost back there?
Sussig: We searched everywhere. Maybe she went away with Raimund.
Flogelind: She wouldn't leave without us. We'll ask for her in the villages. We'll start with this little house.
Misha: What's that on the ground?
Sussig: It's a girl. Is she asleep?
Flogelind: It's the Princess. It's Snow White. *(they gather around her, trying to wake her)*
Sussig: Snow White – oh my goodness – wake up Princess – wake up
Flogelind: *(over-lapping)* Your highness – please wake up –
Misha: *(over-lapping)* Little Princess – little Princess – Is she dead?
Flogelind: *(listening)* Her heart is still beating – very softly – *(**Sussig** runs into the house)*
Sussig: There's no one here *(running out of house)* We have to get some help –

*(**Sussig** runs off in one direction; **Misha** runs off in other direction)*

Sussig/Misha: Help – help – somebody – help –

(They cross the stage calling, exchanging places)

Sussig/Misha: Help – help – somebody – help –
Flogelind: *(during the calling; rocking **Snow White**)* Oh, Princess – wake up – please – Snow White – wake up –

(We hear the running sound of wooden shoes)

Sussig/Misha: *(running in)* Someone's coming – someone's coming –

(The little men rush in led by **Mandel**)

Mandel: What is it? What's happened?
Mertel: The Princess! What have you done to her?
Sussig: No – no – we're her friends – we found her here – lying on the ground.
Misha: She's almost dead – almost – practically –

(They gather around her)

Werther: Her hands are cold –
Steffel: Her pulse is weak –
Wenzel: Could she have eaten something to make her sick?
Stoffel: There're no wounds on her.
Fritz: What's that in her hair?
Mandel: It's only her comb.
Fritz: It isn't hers – she didn't have it before –
Werther: He's right – she didn't –
Stoffel: Here – let me – take – it – out. *(removing it slowly)* There.

*(**Snow White** begins to stir)*

Fritz: She's waking up –
Flogelind: She's all right!
Sussig/Misha: *(hugging each other)* She's all right – she's all right –
Stoffel: It must be a poisoned comb –
Mandel: *(all overlapping)* She could have died –
Mertel: It's lucky you found her –
Werther: She's sitting up –
Steffel: Her pulse is better –
Wenzel: Her color's coming back --
Flogelind: Your highness – can you speak?
Snow White: Oh, Flogelind – Sussig – Misha – you found me –
Sussig: We found you almost dead.
Stoffel: Who gave you this comb?
Snow White: Your friend, Sprinzchen.
The Seven Together: Sprinzchen? Who's she? We don't know any

Sprinzchen. *(ad libs)*
Mandel: I warned you not to talk with strangers.
Snow White: She was so jolly and she said she knew you all and the comb was so pretty –
Misha: Who was she? Why would she hurt you?

(They huddle)

Together: Queen Walpurga Gerhardina Belechech – *(coughing on the last name)*
Mandel: She'll be back. You're not safe here. You must go.
Snow White: Please –let me stay awhile longer – until Raimund comes –
Flogelind: We're here now –
Sussig: We'll protect her –
Misha: We'll stay with her every minute –
Stoffel: Let's get her inside where she can rest.

(They gather around her; lights dim to black)

ACT II Scene 3

*(In the darkness, we hear **Raimund** calling)*

Raimund: Snow White – Snow White – *(Whirlpool spot picks him up)* There has to be a way out of this. Some power stronger than Walpurga's powers. I'm afraid something's happened to Snow White and I can't reach her I don't now if her magical creatures found her. I don't know if it's day or night. But nothing will stop me – I'll find the river of tears and Princess Snow White – *(calling)* Do you hear me Walpurga? Do you hear me?

*(Blackout after first 'Do you hear me' we hear **Walpurga** screech – 'No!' Lights up on dungeon)*

Walpurga: *(yelling at the **Mirror**)* No!! I killed her myself with the poisoned comb. She fell down dead at my feet. She can't still live! She can't!
Hedwig: She can't! She can't!
Mirror: Great enchantress, search again –

>   Snow White's with the little men –
>   The comb is gone from out her hair –
>   Snow White remains above all fair.

Walpurga: AAAAGGGGHHH! *(Hedwig meows & cowers)* If I didn't need your power I'd smash you into pieces –

Hedwig: Try again – try again –

Walpurga: Yes. I will try again, and this time I will not fail. Hedwig – my magic oils –

(Hedwig gives her a flask or pitcher. she pours liquid into the caldron as she speaks)

Walpurga: Caldron churn and caldron change –
>   My gorgeous visage rearrange –
>   A silly hag I'll be instead –
>   I'll be most fair when Snow White's dead!!

(Walpurga, hidden behind smoke, becomes Fritzinn. She laughs wickedly. Black Out)

ACT II Scene 4

(The glen. Snow White is in the house talking softly with Fritz. The little men are getting ready to go back to work giving instructions to Flogelind Sussig & Misha)

Mandel: Now, don't let her out of your sight or out of the house. If this Sprinzchen returns, you know what to do.

(Misha growls)

Flogelind: Poor Misha – he's forgotten how to be fierce.
Steffel: I think I should stay here and help protect the Princess.
Mertel: I'm sure she's perfectly safe now, Walpurga thinks she's dead.
Stoffel: Tomorrow we'll go to the village and get word to her father in the city.
Werther: I'd be glad to escort the Princess to the King.
Wenzel: We should go now – it's almost lunch time.
Mandel: Fritz – we're going now.

*(**Fritz** comes out of the house reluctantly. **Snow White** waves through the open top of the door)*

Fritz: Goodbye, your highness –
Mandel: Stand your guard well.
Flogelind: We will.
Sussig: You can count on us.
Misha: We'll protect her.

*(They march off singing their song. **Snow White** retreats into the house. The 3 creatures take up guarding positions. We hear a light voice singing a silly tune.)*

Fritzinn: *(off)* Night is night and day is day –
  Sad is sad and happy – gay –
  A poem's a poem if it rhymes –
  But I have trouble rhyming mine.

*(**Fritzinn** enters)*

Flogelind: Stop – who are you?
Frizinn: Siste, viator! Hello, bird. Sit tibi terra levis!
Sussig: Who are you?
Misha: What do you want here?
Frizinn: The creatures speak – what fun – what fun – *(claps her hands)*
Flogelind: What do you want?
Frizinn: I don't want anything. Sursum Corda! I have laces to sell – fine wares – siimiplex munditiis!!
Flogelind: We don't need any.
Sussig: What is that you're speaking?
Frizinn: Latin. I've been studying the S's. ; Aren't I clever? *(giggles)*
Misha: Are you Sprinzchen?
Frizinn: Never heard of her. Spero Meliora! I'm Fritzinn. Have we met before? How do you do again. Do you dance?
Sussig: Do we what?
Frizinn: Of course you do; of course you do. *(lines the 3 up)* Now follow me – 1, 2, and a 1 2 3 – 1, 2 and a 1 2 3— again – 1,2 and a 1 2 3 – Tut, tut lion – you're missing all the fun – Come come – Secundum artem – all together – 1, 2 and a 1 2 3 – Very good, very good – Now we sing: Night is night and day is day – Sad is sad and

happy – gay – Keep practicing –keep practicing –1,2 and a 1,2 3-

(She slips into the house; the creatures fumble with the steps)

Snow White: Oh – who are you?
Frizinn: I'm Fritzinn – you lovely thing. Your friends just bought this beautiful bodice for you – *(whips it out of her basket)* Look!!
Snow White: Oh, it's beautiful –
Frizinn: Here, let me help you put it on. Oh what a pretty figure you have – you lucky girl –
Snow White: Oh, thank you –
Frizinn: And we lace it up – like so and like so and like so and like so – there.

*(**Snow White** gasps for air; lets out a little cry & falls down)*

Frizinn: Like so!! *(giggles. She exits the house and crosses quickly to exit)* 1, 2, and a 1 2 3
  Night is night and day is day
  Sad is sad and happy – gay –
  Keep practicing! Keep practicing!

*(Giggles; once off we hear **Walpurga**'s laugh. Hearing the laughter the 3 stop dancing; they look at each other & race into the house)*

Flogelind: Snow White – what has she done to you –
Sussig: What idiots we are – what fools –
Misha: Quickly – let's get her into the fresh air – Carefully – carefully – *(They lift her & carry her out of the house)*
Sussig: She's dead – that silly hag killed her!
Flogelind: While we flitted and danced –

*(**Fritz** enters)*

Misha: Princess – princess –
Fritz: What happened? What happened?
Sussig: A silly hag –
Flogelind: She distracted us –
Misha: She's gone this time –
Fritz: That bodice – she was wearing that – *(he takes it off her)*

Sussig: Quickly – quickly –

*(**Snow White** coughs & sputters & revives as the other Little Men race in)*

Mandel: Did Fritz come back here – he ran out on us – *(seeing **Snow White**)* What happened here?
Mertel: Not again –
Werther: You were guarding her –
Stoffel: You were guarding her –
Fritz: She's all right.

(They gather around her)

Snow White: Why does she hate me so?

(FADE OUT)

ACT II Scene 5

*(**Walpurga**'s dungeon; **Hedwig** & **Mirror** in place)*

Hedwig: Queen of darkness, Queen of death,
Poor Snow White ran out of breath.
Our Walpurga's very glad –
Now Walpurga's truly mad –

*(**Hedwig** hums; **Walpurga** enters)*

Walpurga: I'm exhausted. This has been the most tiresome day. Now that I'm rid of Snow White, I can get my beauty rest. Eudoxia – Euphemia – wake up!
Hedwig: Wake up – wake up –
Walpurga: Now we'll settle this once and for all. Looking glass upon the wall. Who's the fairest of us all?
Mirror: Queen Walpurga be forgiving –
Princess Snow White still is living.
Her friends protect with love and care
Snow White remains above all fair!
Walpurga: AAAGGGGHH! Out of my sight Mirror! Take your sickly powers and go!! I will call on magic that's blacker and stronger

than you!! Go!! I banish you!
Mirror: Do not do this, our great Queen –
We have powers unforeseen –
If you dare us to condemn
Beware!! We'll surely come again!!
Walpurga: Out of my sight!! I'm not afraid of you – I have art beyond you – Go!!

*(**Mirror** leaves; **Walpurga** raises her arms; thunder cracks)*

Walpurga: Invincible demonic power –
I call upon you at this hour –
Provide me magic that will smite –
And rid the world of fair Snow White!!

(Thunder cracks again)

Nothing will ease my anger. I will not rest until
Snow White is gone for good. Until I am again
and forever, the most beautiful of all!!

*(**Walpurga** drinks from one vial, then pours the liquids into the caldron; she shrinks behind the smoke & emerges as **Sigismonda**, holding a bright red apple.)*

Sigismonda: *(shouting)* Snow White!! Nothing will save you now!! *(she laughs wildly)*

BLACK OUT

ACT II Scene 6

*(The glen; twilight; the Seven Little Men are lined up solemnly; they are ready to leave for the mine. **Snow White** is in the house. **Mandel** speaks with **Flogelind, Sussig** & **Misha**)*

Mandel: We won't be long. We'll return in 10 minutes. We have to secure the entrance to our mine. You three guard the exits from the forest. That way no one – not even Walpurga – can enter the

glen.
Flogelind: We won't fail this time.
Sussig: You can trust us.
Misha: We'll guard the Princess well.
Mandel: Soon then —

(They exit singing softly & tiredly; as they leave, the eyes in the moon appear)

Misha: We'd better take up our positions.
Sussig: It'll be dark soon. What will happen then? The queen might get passed us in the dark.
Flogelind: The Seven Little Men will be home before dark. Now — Sussig — you go that way. Misha — that way — I'll keep watch this way. Hurry!

(They hurry off; **Petrus** *&* **Frithmund** *enter, very tired & disheveled)*

Frithmund: It'll be dark soon — then we'll be done for —
Petrus: Frithmund — look — a little house! We're saved! We're saved!
Frithmund: *(hurrying to the house)* We're saved! Please let there be someone home!

(Knocks on the door; **Snow White** *goes to the door tentatively; she doesn't open it)*

Frithmund: Hello? Hello in there! Is anyone home?

*(**Snow White** backs away from the door)*

Petrus: There's no answer — we're lost!
Frithmund: Hello — is anyone home? Hello?
Snow White: Who is it? What do you want?
Frithmund: This is Frithmund —
Petrus: And Petrus from the court of Queen Walpurga —
Snow White: *(to herself)* Petrus — the Queen's chancellor. She must have sent him —
Frithmund: Please let us in. We're tired and hungry —
Petrus: We've been lost in the forest all day —
Snow White: Go away — I can't let you in —

Frithmund: Oh, please – we only want something to eat, a place to rest and directions to the village –
Snow White: Go away –

(The three creatures sneak up behind them)

Petrus: Queen Walpurga will reward you. You can trust us. Open the door –

*(**Misha** growls; **Frithmund** & **Petrus** turn & see the creatures; they scream & run off with the creatures chasing them. **Snow White** listens; the eyes in the moon fade as **Sigismonda** enters)*

Snow White: Thank heavens for Flogelind, Sussig and Misha. The Queen's third plot has failed. I'm safe for a while. Raimund will be here soon, and we'll leave together.

*(**Sigismonda** knocks on the door)*

Snow White: *(runs to door and opens the top of the door)* That must be him!!

*(She sees **Sigismonda** & is frightened)*

Sigismonda: Good evening, dearie. Won't you buy some apples from a poor, old woman?
Snow White: I mustn't buy anything or let anyone in. The seven little men told me not to.
Sigismonda: Suit yourself, dearie. I can sell my beautiful apples elsewhere. See how beautiful?
Snow White: I mustn't buy anything. The seven little men told me not to.
Sigismonda: Suit yourself, dearie. There – I'll give you one.
Snow White: I mustn't take anything.
Sigismonda: *(laughing)* Are you afraid of poison? Tut – tut! I'll cut the apple in half. You can have the rosy side –

*(**Sigismonda** holds the apple up to her while she bites into her half)*

Sigismonda: See? Delicious. Well, do you want it or not? More for me if you don't.

*(**Snow White** reaches out tentatively & takes the apple-half.)*

Snow White: Thank you.

(She bites into it & falls down dead)

Sigismonda: *(laughing)* Thank you, dearie. Finally! The seven little men will not be able to bring you back to life this time. (exiting) Farewell – Snow White!!

BLACK OUT

ACT II Scene 7

Raimund: I don't know how long I've been locked in this strange prison. But now the Circle of Night is getting weaker. I'm able to see a bright light ahead of me. It's a strange, sparking light. And I can hear soft, sad music – it sounds like many people weeping. Listen. Weeping… that means tears. She said the River of Tears would free me from the Circle of Night. I wonder if I've found it. I'll walk toward the light and hope that I'll be free to find Snow White at last.

(He turns)

ACT II Scene 8

*(The Crystal Lake. **Snow White** lies on a bower; sparkling moonlight fills the stage; the Seven Little Men, the 3 creatures, kneel & stand around the dead princess; weeping softly. The Circle of Night fades)*

Raimund: A river of tears. And with good reason. And with good reason. I'm too late. Poor, dear Snow White.

*(He goes to look at her; **Mandel** stops him)*

Mandel: Who are you? What do you want here?

Raimund: I'm Lieber Raimund. I was Snow White's friend.
Mertel: The Princess told us about you. She was waiting for you to come.
Raimund: I'm too late. I was a victim of Walpurga's power –
Werther: So was the Princess.

(Hedwig appears, watching)

Fritz: She looks like the sleeping beauty. She doesn't look dead at all.

(Petrus & Frithmund enter)

Flogelind: It's Walpurga's chancellor and that silly prince –
Misha: I'll get rid of them –

(He approaches them ominously)

Fritz: Wait! Maybe she is like sleeping beauty – Maybe if she's kissed by a prince she'll wake up –
Mertel: Perhaps you're right –
Mandel: *(going to Frithmund)* It probably won't work but it's worth a try. Come on, prince –
Frithmund: Prince? I'm not a prince –
Petrus: Of course you are. Queen Walpurga said there was a prince and a huntsman in the forest.
Frithmund: And I'm the huntsman --
Petrus: Then who's the prin----
Raimund: I'm the prince.
Werther: You certainly aren't dressed like a prince – what are doing wandering around like that?
Raimund: There was trouble in my country. My kingdom is bankrupt – no one has any money. I left to seek my fortune elsewhere so I could return one day and save my kingdom.
Flogelind: Maybe you can save Snow White –
All: Please try –
    Please –
    Save Snow White –
    Save the princess—

(Raimund goes to Snow White; He leans over & kisses her; nothing

happens; everyone begins to weep again)

Raimund: I'm going to take Princess Snow White back to my kingdom and give her a proper burial.

(He begins to lift her; almost drops her; she coughs)

Raimund: *(pointing to a piece of apple on the ground)* Look – a piece of apple was lodged in her throat –
Mandel: Probably poisoned –
Raimund: She's waking up – she's all right!

(All cheer)

Snow White: *(sitting up)* Raimund – I'm so glad to see you.
Raimund: Not as glad as I am. Listen everyone. There's no time to waste. We must leave here at once. When Walpurga discovers that Snow White is still alive, she'll be back with more evil. My country is poor, but it's safe and we'll all be out of Walpurga's reach. And one day – when I restore my kingdom -- perhaps you'll marry me, Snow White.
Snow White: I don't understand what's happened. But I do know that I'll marry you whether you're rich or poor, Raimund.

(The seven little men huddle)

Raimund: Thank you, Princess. And now we must all leave – Gentlemen?

(They come out of the huddle)

Mandel: Prince Lieber Raimund, my brothers and I will come with you to your country.
Mertel: And we'll bring with us all the diamonds from our diamond mine –

*(**Hedwig** sneaks away)*

Stoffel: And we have a lot of diamonds!
Werther: And we'll all be rich!

Wenzel: And we'll all be together!
Fritz: Because we've become very fond of Snow White!

*(All cheer & dance; **Walpurga** & **Hedwig** enter; everyone stops – gasping)*

Walpurga: What a pretty litte party. And no one invited me.
Petrus: Your majesty…..
Walpurga: Silence! Snow White will return to the castle with me – and so will the diamonds. That mine is in my forest.

(All are quaking)

Fritz: *(coming bravely forward)* No, Queen – that mine is part of our glen. You can't have our diamonds.
Raimund: And you can't have Snow White.

*(**Raimund** begins to stalk her, and the others, becoming brave, join him moving forward in a mass)*

Raimund: Go away Walpurga, you have no power here –
All: Go away – go away – go away –

*(**Mirror** creeps up behind **Walpurga**)*

Sussig: This is all you're taking with you, Walpurga!!

*(**Sussig** squirts the queen; all back away from the odor; **Walpurga** falls through the **Mirror** & is immediately locked in the Circle of Night and becomes **Sigismonda**)*

Mirror: Queen, you dared us to condemn –
Triumphantly we've come again!
Beauty belongs to those who care –
Snow White forever is most fair!!
Walpurga: Let me out!! Let me out!! *(she runs off screaming)*

(All cheer)

Mandel: The Queen got what she deserved –
Mertel: Snow White is alive and safe –
Werther: We are all very rich –
Wenzel: And ready for a huge dinner celebration –
Stoffel: We're all making a new start in a new land –
Steffel: Where we'll never have to work again –
Fritz: And we'll be near Snow White –
Flogelind: Who will marry her prince –
Sussig: And live happily –
Misha: Ever –
Snow White/Raimund: After!!!

(All dance and cheer as the curtain falls.)

www.ingramcontent.com/pod-product-compliance
Lightning Source LLC
Chambersburg PA
CBHW071803040426
42446CB00012B/2682